The Vintage Christmas Cookbook

For Amy, with all good wishes for a truly sweet Christmas! Fondly, Angela McRae

The Vintage Christmas Cookbook

A Baby Boomer, Thrifter & Flea Market Fanatic
Shares 25 Old-Fashioned Recipes & Vintage Decor

Angela Webster McRae

Contents

Acknowledgments

A Santa mug full of peppermint candy canes to:

• My truly "sweet" husband, Alex McRae, for spending his spring and summer testing vintage Christmas treats.

• Deberah Williams, friend and book designer extraordinaire, whose talents continue to astonish me. We've been working on projects together for fifteen years now, and she still hasn't figured out how to get rid of me.

• My family and friends who were kind enough to munch some Christmas sweets out of season, including my dad, Buren Webster; sister, Rhonda Horton; and friends Kathy Bohannon and Ruth Schroeder.

• I have too many "enablers" to mention, but a few who deserve a shout-out are Nichole Golden, whose gift of two Santa mugs got the ball rolling (and if you're curious, they appear at top left and bottom right on page 16); Sandra Blair and Joy Breedlove, who delighted me with some much-treasured Christmas tree pins; Monicha Hamil Drew, life-long friend and my "spotter" at area antique malls; Bernideen Canfield, who gave me the treasured gift of a handkerchief from Younker Brothers (pictured on page 30); all of the wonderful Tea With Friends blog readers who have given me Santa mugs over the years; and my late mother and best Santa mug finder, Nancy Webster, who would have gotten such a kick out of this book.

Introduction

I had the good fortune to be born in 1964, what some consider the last year of the Baby Boom, and because of this excellent timing, my childhood Christmases were magical celebrations.

My earliest Christmas photo is a little gem in which my seven-month-old self, festive in my candy-cane-colored pajamas, rides a tricycle in front of a plastic vanity set. A Christmas tree sparkles in the background.

I'm again pictured at Christmas in 1966, now age two and half. I'm wearing a blue polka-dotted housecoat—the same design worn by the Mrs. Beasley doll on the TV show *Family Affair*—and pressing away at my child-sized ironing board, which was the last time I remember enjoying the task of ironing, by the way. I was still an only child at that point, and while I dearly love my sister (waving at Rhonda), ah, those were the days. In a clever bit of foreshadowing, the photo depicts a stack of books perched on the edge of a table, and in the background are not

one but two desks. Anyone who wanted to raise a writer couldn't have selected better gifts.

Before long, I was selecting my own gifts. Like most boys and girls of my era, I practically memorized that gigantic Sears Christmas catalog from the minute it landed in the mailbox each fall. Last year, I was delighted to discover that digital editions of these old catalogs are now available for viewing online (see Resources). Finally, I was able to track down the identity of a doll I had fondly remembered, and now, naturally, I hope to replace her.

When my sister came along eight years after I did, she got indulged with presents too. Board games were frequent gifts throughout our youth, and a favorite family tale

involves the time that Rhonda—who is one of the kindest souls you will ever meet—unwrapped a gift and said, "Yahtzee. Oh boy. Just exactly what I always didn't want." I love that story so much, mainly because there are so many tales involving a cranky me and so few involving a cranky her.

Our family was a typical middle-class American one. Daddy worked at the Ford Motor Company plant in Hapeville, Georgia, and Mama was a homemaker. They made sure we were raised in church and knew that Jesus was "the reason for the season," as we say now, and we didn't have to struggle to keep Christ in Christmas. We knew that without Christ, there was—there is—no Christmas.

When I graduated from college, moved out on my own, and began creating new traditions, I developed a particular fondness for old stuff—or even things that just looked like old stuff. I learned that many of us collect vintage items because we love the history but also, perhaps, because we're trying to recapture a bit of the past.

One reason I enjoy collecting vintage Christmas recipes, ornaments, and decor is that they give me a taste of what Christmas was like when I was a little girl. These charming old things remind me of the times when Christmas meant finally getting to wear my pretty new Christmas dress to church services and then the excitement of desperately trying to go to sleep while waiting on Santa Claus to arrive.

Vintage Christmas recipes help me recall some of these Christmases of yesteryear. These recipes are not particularly sophisticated or upscale. Some involve ordinary ingredients like cornflakes and mashed potatoes. And while I have many Pinterest boards filled with yummy-looking new recipes to try, I don't want the old recipes to disappear.

They remind me of the fun Christmases I enjoyed as a child, and in this day of Instagram-worthy Christmas cakes and TV competitions over who can make the most elaborate sugar cookies, I find it worth remembering that there's nothing wrong with old-fashioned simplicity.

Some of you, I suspect, are my kindred spirits when it comes to celebrating a vintage Christmas. And even if you simply flip through the pages of this book and never cook a thing out of it, I hope you will rediscover a bit of Christmas magic.

It's delightful year-round, yet ambrosia is often reserved as a Christmas treat.

Ageless Ambrosia

Merriam-Webster tells us that "ambrosia" is a noun referring to "the food of the Greek and Roman gods." Daddy tells me it's a food that Grandmama Ruby used to make.

If we started referring to this ageless treat as "Summer Citrus Salad," I'll bet it would be served everywhere from casual eateries like Chick-fil-A and Chicken Salad Chick to the finest restaurants. Instead, it's often reserved as a special Christmas treat, and that's okay too.

In my recipe files, I have a 1931 booklet titled *Coconut Dishes that Everybody Loves*. I have to take exception with that word "everybody," because people are so finicky about coconut these days, but I'll eat their coconut and mine too. The booklet has a recipe for ambrosia, and it calls for just three ingredients: "3 oranges, peeled and thinly sliced, 1/2 cup powdered sugar, 1 can Baker's Coconut, Southern Style." I suppose that's as authentic as it gets, but I like my ambrosia a little fancier than that, so here's how I make it.

2 navel oranges, peeled, pith removed, and cut into chunks
1 (20-ounce) can crushed pineapple, drained and juice reserved
10 Maraschino cherries, chopped in half and rinsed
2 cups sweetened flaked coconut
1/4 cup chopped pecans
1/2 cup confectioners' sugar

In a medium bowl, combine orange chunks, drained pineapple, and cherries. Then add coconut, pecans, and confectioners' sugar and toss. If mixture seems too dry, add a tablespoon or two of reserved pineapple juice to achieve desired consistency. Serve in individual glasses as an elegant dessert. Refrigerate any leftovers. Yields 6-8 servings.

Candy Cane Cookies

It had been years since I'd even thought about making candy cane cookies, then I came across a recipe for them in a 1966 booklet from the Michigan Consolidated Gas Company, a publication that somehow ended up in an antique mall in my town in Georgia.

It was time to give these cookies another try, and boy, are they delicious! I think perhaps it's the addition of both butter and shortening that makes these so light and airy. And when they're fresh out of the oven? Mm, mm, mm.

2-1/2 cups all-purpose flour, sifted
1 teaspoon salt
1/2 cup butter
1/2 cup shortening
1 cup confectioners' sugar, sifted
1 large egg
1-1/2 teaspoons almond extract
1 teaspoon vanilla
1/2 teaspoon red food coloring

Garnish: 1/2 cup crushed peppermint candy mixed with 1/2 cup granulated sugar

Preheat oven to 375 degrees. In a medium-size bowl, sift flour and salt together. In a large bowl, cream butter and shortening, then gradually add the confectioners' sugar. Add egg and flavorings and combine. Fold in dry ingredients and blend well. Divide the dough in half, then add the red food coloring to one half and combine till evenly incorporated throughout the dough. Roll each color of dough into thin strips about 1/4 inch thick

And when they're fresh out of the oven? Mm, mm, mm.

and 5 inches long. Place a red and a white strip side by side, press lightly together, and twist until you're pleased with the spiral design. Place candy canes on ungreased cookie sheet, a few inches apart, forming a short hook at the end of each cookie. Bake for about 9 minutes. (Cookies should be only lightly browned on the bottom.) Immediately sprinkle with peppermint candy/sugar mixture if desired. Yields about 4 dozen cookies.

Cathedral Window Candy

Several variations of this recipe exist, but I like to make it according to the directions I received from the late Joan Chandler. When I was a student at West Georgia College back in the 1980s, I was hired as a student assistant in the music department. The department secretary, Joan Chandler, was my boss and quickly became my friend. (Her name was spelled "Joan" but was pronounced "Joanne." Mrs. Chandler had a twin sister named June, and her mother had wanted both her girls' names to have four letters.)

The music department kept Mrs. Chandler and me plenty busy. If I wasn't typing programs for music recitals or letters for the department chair, I was running errands or delivering messages to the professors. But in between the work, Mrs. Chandler and I became friends, and one Christmas, she shared this delicious treat and recipe with me.

Multicolored marshmallows give this candy its "heavenly" appearance.

I have one caution for you, though: Do not assume that multicolored mini marsh-mallows will always be available when you need them. They will not. White ones, yes. Multicolored, no. I distinctly remember traveling the back roads of West Georgia late one December night in search of the colorful ones, so if you want to make these treats, be sure you've got time to visit a grocery store or two in case your first-choice grocery store is out of multicolored marshmallows.

Mrs. Chandler spends her Christmases in Heaven now, and until we meet again, she's got a permanent place in my heart—and thanks to these heavenly treats, in my recipe files as well.

1 stick butter, softened
1 (12-ounce) package semisweet chocolate chips
1 teaspoon vanilla extract
1 cup chopped pecans
1 package (10 ounces) multicolored miniature marshmallows
1 cup sweetened flaked coconut, divided

In a large saucepan, melt butter and chocolate chips over low heat, stirring constant-ly to prevent scorching. When butter has melted and is thoroughly combined with the chocolate chips, remove pan from heat and stir in vanilla and pecans. Let mixture cool for about 15 minutes but not long enough to thicken.

Fold in the marshmallows and stir until well coated. Using an 18-inch piece of wax paper, spoon half of the mixture lengthwise down the center of the paper. Shape mixture into a log that is approximately 12 x 2 inches. Sprinkle with 1/2 cup of the coconut, evenly coating the outside of the chocolate log.

Wrap the log tightly in the wax paper, folding the ends snugly and tucking them un-der the log. Repeat with the other half of the marshmallow mixture and the remaining coconut. Chill logs in refrigerator until firm, about 2-3 hours or overnight. Unwrap logs and cut into 1/2-inch slices. Yields about 48 large candies.

16

Santa's Merry Mugs

Some years ago, I worked in an office located in the heart of a small downtown in Georgia. Across the street was a tiny little antique shop, and in the window one fall was a display of vintage Santa Claus mugs. I mentioned to my coworker Nichole how cute they were, but I remember thinking that I didn't need to start one more collection.

Hahahahaha.

Nichole gave me two of those wonderful vintage mugs as a Christmas gift that year,

There are lots of fun ways to use your Santa mugs!

and more than 125 Santa mugs later, I'm still collecting them.

My late mother, who I'm convinced could wish things onto the shelves at Goodwill, added many (most?) of the other mugs to my collection. And what a fun collection it is!

For most of the year, they're stored in gigantic plastic crates out in the garage, swathed in a mashup of old newsprint, bubble wrap, and plastic grocery store bags (all items that, I note with interest, may soon be considered collectible in their own right). I have plastic and ceramic mini Santa mugs just over an inch tall, but most of them are in the three- to four-inch-tall range.

One day, I was just in time for a closing sale at an antique store that was going out of business, and there I found a vintage Santa teapot and sugar and creamer, pieces that blend beautifully with the many mugs as well as a few pitchers, candle holders, and other Santa Claus pieces in my collection.

The older Santa mugs, of course, are the ones I like best, and my favorites are the two that were gifts from my friend Nichole.

I'm also fond of the vintage Japanese Santa mugs, which are often about three inches tall and softly faded. These smaller mugs are perfectly suited to all the Christmas teas I drink from late November on.

While I've never bought a Santa mug online, mainly because I've had great luck collecting them offline, I do regularly prowl the online auctions to find information about Santa mugs, which were quite popular in the fifties and sixties.

Ideas for Using Santa Claus Mugs

There are lots of fun ways to use your Santa mugs, and here are a few I like:

* Choose a different Santa mug each week of December and use it exclusively for your coffee, tea, or cocoa that week.

* Instead of a pencil cup, use a Santa mug to display red and green pens and pencils throughout the Christmas season.

* Old-fashioned candy canes from the dollar store make a sweet display when plopped into a Santa mug. I've come across a few solid-white Santa mugs, and when filled with solid-white candy canes, these work well for those who prefer a shabby white palette at Christmas.

* If you've got a chipped or damaged Santa mug you just can't bear to get rid of, use it as the vessel for an arrangement featuring a host of vintage Christmas goodies like mini reindeer, Christmas trees, elves, or snowmen.

* If you're brave enough, you can decorate a large, sturdy artificial Christmas tree using some of your Santa mugs as ornaments. Simply thread the mugs onto branches and twist or hook the branches to secure them in place. Do make sure the tree is extra secure in its base, though, since it could tip over if it shifts from the weight of the mugs. (Ask me how I know. Ahem. But hey, I lost only one!)

* Tuck a Christmas tea towel inside a Santa mug, attach a ribbon and card to the handle, and voila, you have some unique Christmas gift packaging for a hostess gift.

* Hosting a Christmas buffet? Whether you're using vintage silver cutlery or plastic wares in Christmas colors, line them up in a row of vintage Santa mugs.

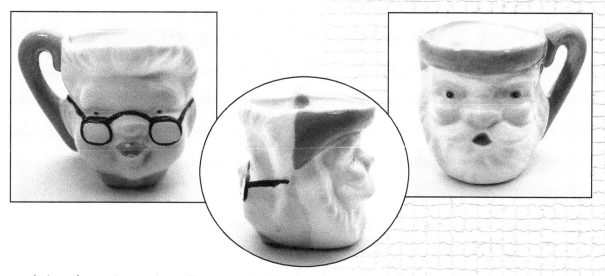

(Above) You know how they say that behind every good man is a good woman? This two-faced Santa mug proves it. While this unmarked mug is somewhat crudely painted, I still find it quite charming and am guessing that it was made in a ceramics class years ago. It's the only one like it that I've come across so far.

(Below) Holt-Howard ceramics were popular in the fifties and sixties, and I believe that my two mini mugs marked 1960-H.H. are some of their work. About ten years ago, these were gifts from one of my blog readers, Carol in Tennessee, who left the price sticker on because she knew I liked bargains. She was right!

I felt proud of myself
the first time I succeeded
in making rosettes.

Christmas Rosettes

A sharp utensil, loose metal parts, and boiling-hot grease. What could go wrong?

When I was researching this book, I came across some old recipes using rosette molds and remembered that I'd bought a set years ago at an antique mall in Alabama. I bought this set because I recalled my mother making rosettes when I was a little girl. Actually, I remember her making them precisely once. And now I'm pretty sure I know why she made them once. They're rather labor intensive, and the first few were sacrificed to the grease gods while I perfected my rosette-dipping technique. There are two important things to remember here: Don't dip the batter any farther than the sides of the mold (you don't want any batter to seep onto the back), and once it's formed, keep the rosette itself in the hot grease just until browned, not burned. If you do this exactly right the first time, you're a better person than I.

I liked the crispy, sweetened rosettes enough to make them twice, and happily, they got easier to make the longer I stayed at it. I had these little guys down to an art form: Dunk mold into batter, dip into grease, listen for grease to "whoosh" for 15 seconds or so, eject, and repeat. Yes, I felt proud of myself the first time I succeeded in making rosettes.

If you happen to have an old rosette mold set and don't have a recipe to use with it, here's the recipe that came with my Party-Patty set, and it served me well.

1 cup sifted all-purpose flour (and sift before measuring)
1/2 cup evaporated milk
1/2 cup water
1 teaspoon sugar
1/2 teaspoon salt
1 large egg, unbeaten

Pour flour into a medium bowl. In smaller bowl, combine evaporated milk, water, sugar, salt, and egg. Slowly stir liquids into the flour, then beat well using an electric mixer until batter is completely smooth. Yields about 30 rosettes.

For safety reasons, I definitely recommend doing a little research and finding the directions specific to your brand of rosette mold. Here are the directions that came with my Party-Patty rosette molds: "Heat mold by dipping into pan of hot fat (365 degrees) for about 10 seconds. Remove mold and shake off excess fat. Dip hot mold into batter, even with the top. No batter should go over top of mold. Dip mold, covered with batter, back into pan of hot fat. As soon as rosette is formed and begins to brown slightly, lift mold and let the rosette drop gently into the hot fat. When rosette is brown on one side, turn it over and brown on other side. Remove from fat and drain on absorbent paper."

Vintage Christmas Handkerchiefs

For many years, I shopped at a place called Collector's Corner, a lovely, sprawling, Victorian-esque antique mall near my house. The building is still there, but Collector's Corner as I once knew it is no more. I can still smell the scent of that wonderful shop whenever I opened the front door to enter it. My favorite place to browse was upstairs, where I never failed to find vendor after vendor offering vintage linens and bone china and old glassware and costume jewelry.

Eventually, I started collecting vintage linens myself, focusing on those with teapot and teacup designs. Many of these designs are quite versatile, and I have a few that I use in my Christmas decor. That's fortunate, because on my jaunts to antique malls and thrift stores, I haven't had much luck finding Christmas tablecloths and tea towels in good condition. I'm determined to keep searching for a deal, though. But there's one type of vintage linen that I have had success finding, and that's the vintage Christmas handkerchief.

I know, I know. You can't dwell on the hankie's original use. But as long as your hankies are washed, pressed, and dolled up for the Christmas table, why not use them as napkins? I do.

29

I realized one day that, without even meaning to, I had collected about a dozen poinsettia-print vintage hankies. The designs are so cheerful and charming, and I use them to line tea trays or drape across a basket. They're a little thin to stand up well in napkin rings, but you can easily slip vintage handkerchiefs through the handle of a teacup. I also like to borrow from another of my favorite Christmas collectibles, vintage Christmas tree pins, and use beribboned pins to fashion "napkin rings" that truly sparkle on the table. (They say that silver is the jewelry of the table, but let me go on record as saying I'm a fan of using actual jewelry on the table.)

Vintage handkerchiefs are also great tuck-ins for Christmas cards. They can be slipped under a package's ribbon for an extra splash of color. Another fun idea is to wrap a mini-sized Bundt cake in plastic wrap, then center it in the middle of a vintage handkerchief and secure the cake safely inside by tying the hankie with a ribbon. Party favors, anyone?

I can't think of a simpler, sweeter Christmas collectible than Christmas hankies, and if you know someone who collects them, they're great gifts all their own.

I use them to line
tea trays or drape
across a basket.

Merry Christmas Cookies

I don't mean to belabor the point, but I don't understand why so many people insist they don't like coconut.

Coconut features in a lot of great sweets—ambrosia, macaroons, and coconut cake come to mind—and these cookies are another fine way to use coconut in your Christmas cooking. This recipe comes from a vintage ad for Baker's Coconut, and they called these Merry Christmas Cookies. They're made even more festive with colored icing and sprinkles of coconut.

1-1/2 cups all-purpose flour
1-1/2 teaspoons baking powder
1/4 teaspoon salt
1 cup sugar
1/2 cup shortening
2 eggs, unbeaten
1/4 cup milk, divided use
1 teaspoon vanilla
1-1/2 cups shredded coconut, plus extra for garnish

Sift flour, then measure it. Add baking powder, salt, and sugar and sift again into a mixing bowl. Add shortening, eggs, 2 tablespoons of the milk, and vanilla and beat for 2 minutes with an electric mixer. Add coconut and remaining milk and beat for another half minute on low speed of mixer. Chill batter in refrigerator for 2 hours, then drop by teaspoonfuls onto ungreased cookie sheets. Bake at 400 degrees for 10 minutes or until cookies are lightly browned on the edges. When cookies have cooled, ice as desired and sprinkle with more coconut. Yields about 6 dozen cookies.

Icing: For each color of icing, combine 1 cup of confectioners' sugar with 1-2 tablespoons of milk and tint with food coloring as desired.

These festive cookies feature colored icing and coconut sprinkles.

Mexican Spiced Nuts

At a local antique store one day, I came upon a sweet stash of vintage Christmas recipe booklets, and this is another one from the Michigan Consolidated Gas Company and includes a 1958 calendar and a recipe for Mexican Spiced Nuts. The recipe makes two cups of nuts, a great gift when presented in a pretty glass jar or canister. If you're preparing baskets or trays of Christmas treats for several friends, as I sometimes do, you could add a small amount of these (just enough to fill a paper mini-muffin cup) and share a sampling with several recipients. Or you could eat 'em all yourself, which is what you're going to want to do because these are THAT good.

3 cups confectioners' sugar
1/4 cup cornstarch
1 teaspoon salt
2 teaspoons cinnamon
1/2 teaspoon allspice
1/2 teaspoon chili powder
1/2 teaspoon cloves
2 egg whites
1/4 cup cold water
2 cups pecan or walnut halves (I used 1 cup of each)

Preheat oven to 250 degrees. (That's 250, with a "2.") Sift dry ingredients together in a large bowl. In a smaller bowl, beat egg whites slightly and add the cold water. Dip each nut in the egg white and water mixture, then drain on

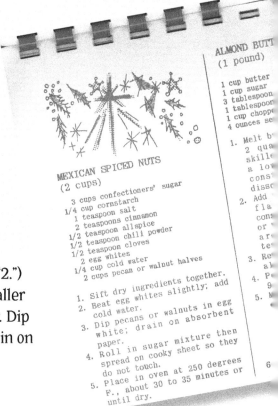

MEXICAN SPICED NUTS
(2 cups)

3 cups confectioners' sugar
1/4 cup cornstarch
1 teaspoon salt
2 teaspoons cinnamon
1/2 teaspoon allspice
1/2 teaspoon chili powder
1/2 teaspoon cloves
2 egg whites
1/4 cup cold water
2 cups pecan or walnut halves

1. Sift dry ingredients together.
2. Beat egg whites slightly; add cold water.
3. Dip pecans or walnuts in egg white; drain on absorbent paper.
4. Roll in sugar mixture then spread on cooky sheet so they do not touch.
5. Place in oven at 250 degrees F., about 30 to 35 minutes or until dry.

ALMOND BUTT
(1 pound)

1 cup butter
1 cup sugar
3 tablespoon
1 tablespoon
1 cup choppe
4 ounces se

1. Melt b
  2 qua
  skille
  a lo
  cons
  dissc
2. Add
  fla
  cons
  or
  a r
  te
3. Re
  a
4. P
  9
5. N

6

a paper towel. Roll each nut in the confectioners' sugar mixture until coated well, rolling them twice if necessary to absorb the sugar and spices. Space nuts apart on a cookie sheet lined with aluminum foil or parchment and bake for 30-35 minutes or until dry. Yields 2 cups.

Christmas Greetings

IGAN CONSOLIDATED GAS COMPANY

Makes great gifts and snacks!

PINEAPPLE SQUARES
(Makes 4 dozen - 1 inch pieces)

4 envelopes gelatin
2 cups sugar
2 tablespoons cornstarch
1/4 teaspoon salt
2-1/2 cups crushed pineapple
      (Number 2 can)
3 tablespoons lemon juice
1/2 cup finely chopped nuts
Green or red vegetable coloring
Confectioners' sugar

1. Combine gelatine, sugar, cornstarch and salt in saucepan.
2. Add pineapple, blend well.
3. Bring to a boil over a medium gas flame. Boil for 20 minutes.
4. Add lemon juice, nuts and few drops vegetable coloring.
5. Pour into an aluminum foil lined 8 inch square pan. Allow to cool overnight.
6. Loosen around edges and turn out onto confectioners' sugar covered board.
7. Peel off foil and cut in 1 inch cubes.
8. Roll in confectioners' sugar.

n a
n a
over
ring
r is

rease
rring
ees F.
is that
e when
ater.
1/2 cup

buttered

late and
   Sprinkle
ng toasted
r half of
at process
   chocolate
irst side.
is hardened
ieces.

Chocolate Peppermint Brownies

When it comes to the world of antiquing, I've learned that many of us regret the things that we *didn't* buy more than the things that we did buy.

Years ago, I was at an antique mall in Marietta, Georgia, when I came across a stash of vintage *American Cookery* magazines. They were just a few dollars each, but I bought only a couple of them. Now, I wish I'd bought every one they had. My favorite is the December 1939 issue, the cover of which features a poinsettia salad made of cooked apples. Inside is a recipe for Chocolate Peppermint Brownies, and they're simply delicious. That half a teaspoon of peppermint flavoring is just enough to give these brownies a little Christmas pizzazz. If you're a fan of peppermint, too, put these on your to-try list.

3/4 cup all-purpose flour
1/2 teaspoon baking powder
1/2 teaspoon salt
1/3 cup butter
2 squares unsweetened chocolate, melted (I used Baker's Unsweetened Chocolate Baking Bar and broke off two of the 1/4-ounce squares)
1 cup sugar
2 eggs, well beaten
3/4 cup chopped walnuts
1/2 teaspoon peppermint extract

Preheat oven to 350 degrees. In a mixing bowl, sift together the flour, baking powder,

Peppermint flavoring + brownies = Christmas pizzazz!

and salt and set aside. In separate bowl, add the butter to the melted chocolate and blend well. In another bowl (I know this is a lot of bowls, but hey, this is how the magazine said to do it), add the sugar to the eggs and beat, then add the chocolate mixture and combine. Add the dry ingredients to the wet ingredients, then add the nuts and peppermint extract and combine. Pour into a greased eight-inch-square baking dish and bake for 35 minutes. Remove brownies from oven, let cool, and cut in squares. Yields 16 large or 25 small brownies.

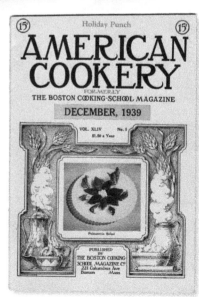

Holiday Punch
15¢   15¢
AMERICAN COOKERY
FORMERLY
THE BOSTON COOKING-SCHOOL MAGAZINE
DECEMBER, 1939
VOL. XLIV   No. 5
$1.50 a Year

Poinsettia Salad

PUBLISHED BY
THE BOSTON COOKING-SCHOOL MAGAZINE Co
221 Columbus Ave
Boston   Mass

Classic Cornflake Candy

The early seventies? That's my best estimate for when I first enjoyed cornflake candy. I recall my mother making it in the house I grew up in, and since this is a four-ingredient recipe and my mother didn't particularly enjoy cooking, no wonder she liked it. It was easy, foolproof, and delicious.

Please don't gussy it up too much!

Food history sites don't yet seem to recognize cornflake candy as worthy of documenting (their loss), so I'll just say this: Kellogg's Corn Flakes came along in 1894, and my guess is that some enterprising housewife with a sweet tooth developed this recipe not long afterward. Or maybe it was a Depression-era mother wanting sweet treats for her children at Christmas.

What I do know is this: If you want authentic cornflake candy, please don't gussy it up too much. I know, I know. The temptation is there. I've seen add-ins of butterscotch morsels, chocolate chips, various nuts, and even a teaspoon of vanilla. While I understand the temptation to use *crunchy* peanut butter (hey, it's my favorite too), I recommend using the creamy. Some people commit cornflake candy sacrilege and crunch up the poor little dears by making tiny, tight little balls out of this mixture, but then we can't be responsible for those who weren't raised right, can we?

The worst cornflake candy corruption I've seen, however, came when one modern-day maker topped hers with red and green candy sprinkles. It's enough to make a Baby Boomer weep. Stop it, y'all. Let's save the cornflake candy. And enjoy!

1 cup granulated sugar
1 cup light corn syrup
1 cup creamy peanut butter
5 cups cornflake cereal

Pour sugar and corn syrup into a medium saucepan, stir, and cook gently over medium heat. When mixture is approaching the boiling point (yes, over medium heat), turn off heat and add peanut butter. Blend well. Quickly pour mixture into a large mixing bowl and add cereal a cup or two at a time. Combine well and make sure that all cornflakes are covered with the mixture. I blend mine with a rubber spatula so as not to smoosh the cornflakes. Drop by tablespoons onto wax paper and allow to firm before serving. Yields about 50 pieces of candy.

A recipe found on
old handwritten
recipe cards

Creamy Egg Nog

This recipe is an anonymous one I found on one of those websites that shares old handwritten recipe cards and basically says, "Good luck!" My first attempt at this egg nog, which originally called for 4 cups of milk, was too thin. The drink was tasty but not as thick as I wanted. I found that substituting cream for one of the cups of milk made for a richer, more milkshake-like drink. I've since learned that some egg nog aficionados believe it's okay to substitute even more cream for the milk, but let's not go crazy here.

1/3 cup sugar
2 eggs, yolks and whites separated for divided use*
1/4 teaspoon salt
3 cups milk
1 cup heavy whipping cream
3 tablespoons sugar
1 teaspoon vanilla
Optional: Nutmeg for garnish

In a medium saucepan, beat the 1/3 cup sugar into the egg yolks. Add salt, then stir in the milk and cream. Cook over medium heat, stirring constantly until mixture coats spoon. Cool and set aside. In separate bowl, beat egg whites until foamy and gradually add the remaining sugar, beating until soft peaks form. Add to custard and mix thoroughly. Add vanilla, blend, and chill for three or four hours before serving. Garnish with nutmeg if desired. Yields 4-6 servings.

Please note that I used pasteurized eggs, which are recommended in foods like this one since the egg whites aren't cooked prior to their addition.

Easy Toffee

Back when I was a newspaper feature writer, I interviewed a local woman who had written a book, and her best friend was there for the interview. The two were a lot of fun, and they were just bowled over by a recipe they'd come across for a chocolate candy that included saltines as an ingredient.

It would be a few years before I made the recipe for myself, and it's now one of my all-time favorite easy recipes. I've heard these toffee candies called "Christmas crack" and other less-than-savory names, but I'm going with "Easy Toffee."

24 saltines
1 stick butter
1/2 cup packed brown sugar
1 cup semisweet chocolate chips
1/2 cup pecans or other nuts, as desired

Preheat oven to 350 degrees. Line a cookie sheet with aluminum foil and arrange saltines in four rows of six crackers each. Fold foil tightly around edges of saltines to create a "rim" for the foil. Melt butter and brown sugar in microwave and combine well. Pour mixture over saltines, bake for five minutes, and remove pan from oven. Sprinkle chocolate chips over hot saltines and allow to soften on stovetop for about two minutes, then spread chocolate evenly over saltines. Sprinkle with pecans and let the toffee cool in refrigerator for an hour or two before serving. Break into pieces and try not to scarf it down in one sitting.

One of my all-time favorite easy recipes

One of my favorite
Christmas recipes from the
Halle Brothers Company

Halle's Cranberry Bread

Some of my earliest Christmas memories are of going to Atlanta to shop at both Davison's and Rich's department stores. I sure miss them. I love this country's grand old department stores and have made a hobby of researching recipes from their restaurants and tearooms. In 2011, I published my first book, *Dainty Dining*, which features recipes from some of these old stores. What a lovely surprise it was to discover that readers all across the country share my fondness for old department stores and their foods.

I continued to search for recipes from old department stores after the book was published, and one of my favorites is a Christmas recipe from a store in Cleveland, Ohio, the Halle Brothers Company. Oscar-winning actress Halle Berry was named after this department store, and curiously enough, when she was in college, she worked for the Cleveland store that was one of Halle Brothers' competitors, the Higbee Company. (The Higbee department store is where little Ralphie in *A Christmas Story* first lusted over that Red Ryder BB gun in the window.)

When I learned that a book of the old store's favorite holiday recipes was published in 1999, I eagerly snagged a copy on eBay. Since I adore the tart flavor of cranberries, I had to try the Halle's Cranberry Bread, and it has become a favorite Christmas treat and one of the holiday foods I make most often.

I like to bake this cranberry bread in mini loaves to give as gifts. You can bake the recipe in three mini (3 x 5-inch) loaf pans to share with several friends, or for one deluxe gift, bake it in a 9 x 5 x 3-inch loaf pan, cover with plastic wrap, and send it off with a pretty tea towel and ribbon.

2 cups all-purpose flour
1 cup granulated sugar
1-1/2 teaspoons baking powder
1/2 teaspoon baking soda
1 teaspoon salt
Juice and zest of 1 orange
2 tablespoons shortening
1/2 cup plus 2 tablespoons boiling water
1 egg, beaten
1 cup chopped pecans
1 cup fresh cranberries, cut in halves

Sift together flour, sugar, baking powder, baking soda, and salt. In separate large bowl, combine juice and orange zest, shortening, boiling water, and egg. Add dry ingredients to the liquid ones and blend just until combined. Add pecans and cranberries and mix well. Pour into pan (or pans) prepared with cooking spray. Allow batter to stand for 20 minutes before baking. Bake at 350 degrees for 60-70 minutes or until a knife inserted in the center comes out clean. (Bake for only 50 minutes if you're baking mini loaves.) Yields 1 large loaf or 3 mini loaves.

47

A Rushton
Santa, the
doll of my
dreams

48

The Santa from Atlanta

So I got a bee in my bonnet that I needed a vintage Santa doll.

It was the kind of piece that I wasn't in any particular hurry to acquire, just a loosely envisioned "want" that was on my collectibles bucket list.

One day a few years ago, I was shopping at an antique mall in a nearby town when I saw him. You know that scene in *A Christmas Story* where Ralphie imagines the teacher's reaction to his composition? As the music crescendos, she exults over "the theme I've been waiting for all my life!"

The music might have been a little softer there at the antique mall, but I'm pretty sure I heard it when I came across the sixteen-inch-tall stuffed Santa doll. Every junker knows the thrill of the hunt and the trepidation of reaching for the price tag. Would it be marked "NFS," not for sale? Would it be a hundred dollars? Would they give me ten percent off?

Reader, Santa was on sale for eight dollars.

I got a little nervous when a hanger-on near the register asked to see my Santa doll and seemed a little too impressed with my bargain. Let's just say that I was looking over my shoulder when I got in my car.

I loved-loved-loved the look of my vintage doll, and when I got home, I searched him for any identifying

marks. Would you believe he was a Rushton Santa!

Well, okay, I'll admit that I'd never heard of a Rushton Santa before that day, but I learned fast. It seems these dolls had their heyday in the fifties and sixties, and many of them had rubber faces, hands, and feet. Mine has a tag that says, "The Rushton Company, Atlanta, GA." Some of these dolls were sold at my beloved (and sadly, gone) Rich's Department Store in Atlanta.

Only when I got my Santa doll home did I notice that one hand was empty but appeared to have a space to hold something. A bag of toys, maybe? Further investigation revealed that he originally held a miniature Coca-Cola bottle. And guess what I just happened to have sitting

50

around in a desk drawer—a miniature Coca-Cola bottle that was the perfect size. I've never collected Coca-Cola memorabilia, so I have no idea how I ended up with that, but I'm glad I did.

Some things are meant to be.

My Rushton Santa doll is one of my favorite Santa collectibles, and now I enjoy acquiring other old Santas. Last year, I shared

my vintage Christmas obsession with an old friend, and before I knew it, Monicha was texting me photos of plastic garland and satin ornaments and other delights to see if I wanted them. (Yes and yes and yes.)

When I met her for the pickup, she surprised me with a gift of a Santa I'd never seen before, a wind-up tin Santa that looks as old as Methuselah. I absolutely love him—and I love that a childhood friend spotted him for me.

Other toy Santas are making their way into my collection, too, from a tiny flocked Santa to a cute plastic one with a sleigh and reindeer.

Santa is truly the gift that keeps on giving!

51

Haystacks

Don't all of you go rushing up there or anything, but Wisconsin is a great place to go junkin'.

I wasn't sure what to think about the Cheese State when my stepdaughter, Heather, married her beau, Brad, a Wisconsin native, and moved up north. I have since become quite the fan of not only Brad and his delightful, salt-of-the-earth Wisconsin family but also of all the pleasures their state has to offer, not least of which is the pleasant summer and fall weather. I've been to a fish boil in Egg Harbor, behind the scenes at a dairy farm near Green Bay, and even—hold on to your cheese-wedge hat—to a Packers football game at Lambeau Field, or as my husband refers to it when we're up there, "the Vatican."

Wisconsin is also, I have discovered, a treasure trove of thrift stores, antique malls, and garage sales. I have returned to Georgia with goodies from all of them. At the thrift stores, I can't resist buying the vintage recipe booklets I've found there for just pennies, including one from the Wisconsin Gas Company. In it was a recipe for something called Tingalings. It called for butterscotch chips and chow mein noodles and peanuts, a recipe that seemed so familiar I could taste it, but the name wasn't familiar. Then I had a eureka moment and thought, "Haystacks!"

These Haystacks are one of the finest three-ingredient recipes I know, and if you haven't made good old-fashioned Haystacks in a while, give them a try.

1 (11-ounce) bag butterscotch chips
1 cup peanuts
2 cups chow mein noodles

Using a double boiler over medium heat, slowly melt the butterscotch chips. Add the peanuts and, carefully using a wooden spoon or rubber spatula, stir to coat. Then add the chow mein noodles and, again, stir with a light hand so as not to crunch the noodles while making sure they're covered in butterscotch. Drop by teaspoons full onto wax paper and allow to cool completely. Yields 36 Haystacks.

Haystacks are one of the finest three-ingredient recipes I know.

This hot chocolate recipe
has a secret ingredient—
peppermint patties!

Hot Mint Chocolate

You've probably got a favorite hot chocolate recipe, even if it looks something like this: "Carefully tear open the packet of Swiss Miss and ..."

But if you don't have a favorite hot chocolate recipe, and if you're a fan of mint like I am, then do yourself a favor and try this recipe featured in a 1966 booklet from the Michigan Consolidated Gas Company. This recipe stars peppermint patties and gives you a good excuse to buy a bagful. Then you can eat any leftovers.

20 chocolate-covered mint patties, 1-1/2 inch in diameter (I used York Peppermint Patties)
3 cups milk, divided use
1/8 teaspoon salt
1 cup light cream

In a medium saucepan over low heat, combine mint patties, one cup of the milk, and the salt. Stir constantly until the candies are melted and the mixture is blended well. Add the remaining milk and the cream and continue to stir. Heat until the hot chocolate is scalding hot. Serve with whipped cream if desired. Yields 10 one-half cup servings.

Market Bulletin Orange Balls

Like many cooks of her era, Grandmother Doris clipped recipes from the *Farmers and Consumers Market Bulletin*, aka the *Market Bulletin*, a publication of the Georgia Department of Agriculture. When I came across her yellowed clipping for these yummy little orange balls years ago, I began making them at Christmas. They're a snap to make and a joy to eat.

The refrigerated, bite-sized treats get their texture from vanilla wafer crumbs and pecans. The citrus flavor from the frozen orange juice is a nice switch from the heavier sweets you often find at Christmas. And if you don't need to make these as Christmas treats, you might want to try them on a tea tray sometime.

1 (16-ounce) box plus 1 cup powdered sugar, divided use
1/2 cup butter or margarine, softened
1 (6-ounce) can frozen orange juice (DO NOT THAW)
1 (12-ounce) box vanilla wafers, crushed in food processor
1 cup chopped pecans

Combine the 16-ounce box of powdered sugar, butter, frozen orange juice, vanilla wafers, and pecans. Mixture will be very stiff. Shape into balls about the size of a large gumball and roll in remaining 1 cup of powdered sugar. Store in refrigerator. Yields about 5 dozen Orange Balls.

They're a snap to make and a joy to eat.

Vintage Christmas China, Ceramics, and Glassware

Because I'm a tea lover and enjoy having friends over for Christmas tea, I'll never, ever have too much Christmas china. I'll buy any vintage Christmas teacup I find that's reasonably priced. I also look for tidbit trays, candy dishes, and other Christmas serving pieces as I come across them. Occasionally, I discover vintage Christmas ceramics like boots, sleighs, and Santa-shaped banks and jars. These are great double-duty items since they can be both decor and serving piece. My vintage sleigh with spaghetti trim, a seventy-nine-cent find from the Salvation Army, has been called into duty for serving up both my Orange Ball and Peanut Butter Ball treats.

So Christmas tea wares are always on my to-be-bought list, but there's another very important reason I won't stop looking for Christmas china and glassware.

I'll never forget the December evening that I

59

stood in a grocery store aisle, looking at the picked-over plastic wares so that I could buy one to transport some Christmas treats as a last-minute gift for someone. A lone round plastic tray was left. It was hideous. It had no design and, while it was new and had the label on it, was scratched all to pieces. But I was in a bind, because I had to have something to transport the Christmas treats on, and I hadn't planned ahead. What galled me most was that I had to pay five dollars for the privilege of schlepping that ugly plastic platter

home with me.

Oh, sure, slap a pretty paper doily on anything and it will work, but that's beside the point. All I could think of was all the gorgeous Christmas plates and platters I'd left at antique malls and thrift stores that year.

Right then and there, I made up my mind: Never again. As Scarlett O'Hara might have said, "As God is my witness, I'll never give Christmas treats on ugly plastic again."

And so the search began. I've found gorgeous gilded-edge Limoges plates for a dollar at a yard sale. At the Salvation Army, I found an old Mikasa crystal platter in mint condition for fifty cents (it's displaying the Orange-Slice Bars in this book). Goodwill? They have inexpensive vintage Christmas plates all year

61

long, and I found two huge ones with poinsettias on them for a dollar each.

These days, I don't just limit myself to Christmas designs when I'm shopping for plates and platters to give away. I like to share food gifts all year long, so I'll buy any pretty vintage plate that's a dollar or two.

The only problem is that the recipient sometimes wants to give the plate back, but once I emphasize that I shopped at thrift stores, that seems to make the "extravagance" okay.

When shopping, I look for these plates and platters first, but ceramics are next on the list. Vintage Christmas pieces with an open top can also be used to hold flatware or flowers at a Christmas tea, so I'm always happy to find these whimsical old ceramic wares. If you begin to think of them as "tablescape" material, so will you.

Occasionally, I discover vintage Christmas ceramics like boots.

Orange-Slice Bars

Quick: What's your favorite childhood candy? If you're a fellow Baby Boomer, your favorite sweet treat from yesteryear may be something that's hard to come by, like Astro Pops (my personal fave) or Mary Janes, Tootsie Rolls, Sugar Babies, Fireballs, Shoestring Licorice, Pom Poms, Candy Corn, Pixie Sticks, or Clove Life Savers (some of my friends' faves when I asked on Facebook).

One old-time candy that's always easy to find is orange-slice candy. Those sugary gumdrop-like treats seem to pop up in every grocery store, convenience store, and big-box store in America, and I'm wondering who's buying the things. It's not that they're bad. No, it's more that there are so many candies that are better, like Astro Pops, for instance. If you had to retire a candy, why not send orange slices on to the great Candyland game in the sky? If I were queen, I would say let's keep those star-shaped nonpareils that I can never find anymore, and orange slices could be special ordered through some pricy online vendor. Can I get an amen?

But lest you think I am *completely* opposed to orange-slice candy when I most certainly am not, I present to you these yummy Orange-Slice Bars, courtesy of a 1950s issue of *Woman's Day* magazine.

The size of the bag of candy had to be adjusted. Apparently, a 16-ounce bag of orange-slice candy was common in the fifties. Nearly seventy years on down the road, a 10-ounce bag is all you'll find. As this original recipe made two pans of candy, I halved it, which made the 10-ounce bag just fine for my purposes.

1 (10-ounce) bag candy orange slices, reserving 5 or 6 pieces for garnish
1 cup sifted all-purpose flour
1/4 teaspoon salt
1-1/2 cups light brown sugar, packed

2 eggs, slightly beaten
1/2 cup chopped nuts (I used pecans)
1/2 teaspoon vanilla

Preheat oven to 350 degrees. With a sharp knife or kitchen shears dipped in cold water, cut orange slices into small pieces. (I chopped mine into 6 or 7 pieces each.) Pour flour into a medium bowl, add salt and chopped candies, and toss. Add remaining ingredients and blend till everything is combined well. You will have a stiff, sticky batter. Spoon batter into a 9-inch-square baking pan coated with cooking spray or lined with parchment. Bake for 40-45 minutes and cool in pan. Cut into 1 x 3-inch bars. (The original recipe said you could roll these bars in fine granulated sugar if desired, but I found they were perfect as they were.)

Made with an easy-to-find old-time candy.

Peanut Butter Balls

Yes, I'm aware that in Ohio and other places, they leave some peanut butter showing and call these treats "Buckeyes," but I live in an SEC-loving household, so we call them "Peanut Butter Balls."

And speaking of the SEC, I'm pretty sure I was first introduced to Peanut Butter Balls about forty years ago, at a Sugar Bowl party on New Year's Day in 1981. Some of my high school classmates and I had gathered at a friend's house to watch the game pitting the University of Georgia against Notre Dame. First, we pigged out on salty and sweet snacks, including homemade Peanut Butter Balls, and then we watched the game. I still remember everyone's excitement as we followed Herschel Walker as he rushed down the field for the Bulldogs, and UGA won the title! This particular memory is rather remarkable to me since I'm not even a big football fan, but I do still admire Herschel Walker.

And I still love Peanut Butter Balls. Some cooks these days are dressing them up with chocolate drizzles and such, but I like mine simple.

Go Dawgs!

1/2 cup creamy peanut butter
6 tablespoons softened butter, divided use
1 cup confectioners' sugar
1 cup semisweet chocolate chips
1 tablespoon hot water

In small bowl of an electric mixer, combine the peanut butter and 3 tablespoons of the butter and blend well. Gradually add the confectioners' sugar and combine. Allow peanut butter mixture to chill in refrigerator or freezer for 30 minutes, then scoop by teaspoons and roll into pieces about the size of a large gumball.

For chocolate dip: Feel free to use your favorite chocolate dip recipe using chocolate chips, but here's the one that works for me. Melt chocolate chips and remaining 3 tablespoons of butter in a double boiler (or microwave) and add the tablespoon of hot water. Blend well until mixture is smooth. Dip balls of peanut butter mixture into the chocolate dip using a fork* and tap on side of bowl or on a piece of wax paper to remove excess. Place dipped balls on wax paper, refrigerate, and allow to harden. Refrigerate any leftovers. Yields about 30 Peanut Butter Balls.

Tip: *For easy dipping of chocolates, use a plastic fork with four tines and break off the middle two. You'll have an easy-to-use tool for dipping candy.*

Introduced to me at a Sugar Bowl party ... a treat you'll love.

Religious figures
are hard to come by
when shopping for
vintage Christmas
decorations.

"oh" is for ornaments

Few things ring my bell, if you will, more than finding a pretty vintage Christmas ornament. Earlier this year, it came in the form of a delightfully kitschy plastic bell, all cheap glitter and flocked velvet and absolutely no taste. I couldn't love it more.

How did I find it? I happened to be speaking to my friend Lorelle's garden club on the subject of tea that morning, and afterward, the two of us decided to visit a local antique mall, the perfect way to spend an afternoon. Lorelle and I went to college together, and in recent years, we had socialized only at funerals (welcome to middle age!), but we gathered for a thoroughly happy reason that day. In the back of my mind, though, I wondered, "Can I shop with Lorelle?" I'd never shopped with Lorelle before. I generally shop alone, and shopping with another woman is always an iffy proposition.

Lorelle, it turned out, was my kind of shopping companion, and I learned that she is a wanderer/browser just like I am. In fact, we found a stack of vintage Christmas carol booklets that were duplicates, and we both bought one. So when I got home from that exceptionally lovely day, I thought of her when I unpacked what I now think of as my "Lorelle bell" ornament. I truly believe that certain friends bring us luck.

But this wasn't my first plastic ornament. Years ago, I was at a local second-hand shop when I found a cardboard box containing four plastic ornaments, with two featuring a chorus of four little boys and two featuring the Holy Family. Religious figures are oddly hard to come by when I'm shopping for vintage Christmas decorations, and goodness knows I need the Lord's reminders to help me get through the Christmas season with my focus where it ought to be. In Jan Mitford's wonderful Christmas novel, *Shepherds Abiding*, Father Tim Kavanagh restores a vintage nativity set as a marvelous surprise for his wife, Cynthia. In my dreams, I will come across just such a set at Goodwill one day.

Meanwhile, I continue to prowl thrift stores and antique malls for vintage ornaments. I've had some success finding eighties- and nineties-era teacup and teapot ornaments, perhaps because I've developed a good tea radar over the years. Not long ago, I visited a new-to-me thrift store out of town and came across a 1980s Hallmark Keepsake teacup ornament, still in the original box and in mint condition. It was only forty-nine cents, and then I got to the checkout counter and learned it was half off.

That was one of the best quarters I spent all year. I now have more than a hundred teapot and teacup ornaments, and the oldest ones are my favorites.

You know what I think are going to be the most collectible ornaments in the years ahead? Anything Hallmark, of course; anything depicting Christmas movies like *A Christmas Story, Elf,* and *Christmas Vacation*; anything *Star Wars*; and if I were investing in ornaments for the future, I'd probably pick up a few extra red pickup trucks with a Christmas tree strapped in back. Those ornies have been everywhere in recent years. Fifty years from now, I just know that someone will pick up a tiny pickup and say, "Ah, yes, the early 2000s!"

Collecting vintage ornaments is fun but can take a while, so if possible, begin yesterday. I sure wish I had.

Peanut Butter Cookies

Whenever I find old cookbooks and recipe booklets, I look for the most grease-stained, splattered, and unpristine page in the whole book. That tells me the recipe is a good one, and that's the one I want to make.

Festive Foods: A Treasury of Holiday Treats from the Milwaukee Gas Light Company is a 1962 booklet that was one of my Wisconsin thrift store finds. The page with their peanut butter cookie recipe is splattered with what I imagine was shortening or butter, and on seeing it, I started thinking about peanut butter cookies, which I had not previously considered for this book. Aren't those too ordinary? Besides, in recent years, I've been making those newer three-ingredient peanut butter cookies (1 cup peanut butter, 1 cup sugar, 1 egg, bake at 350 degrees for 6-8 minutes, and done).

But then I thought about those old-timey Peanut Butter Cookies, lovingly made from scratch, rolled in sugar, and pressed with the tines of a fork. So I made some, and the minute I put one of these hot-from-the-oven cookies in my mouth, it tasted like Christmas all over again.

> **1-3/4 cups all-purpose flour**
> **1 teaspoon baking soda**
> **1/2 teaspoon salt**
> **1/2 cup peanut butter**
> **3/4 cup shortening**
> **1/2 cup brown sugar, packed**
> **1/2 cup granulated sugar plus extra for rolling**
> **1 egg**

Preheat oven to 350 degrees. In a medium bowl, sift together the flour, soda, and salt and set aside. In a large bowl, cream the peanut butter and shortening. Gradually add the sugars and mix until fluffy. Add egg and blend well. Finally, add sifted ingredients and combine. Shape dough into gumball-sized pieces and roll in granulated sugar. Space two inches apart on ungreased cookie sheet and make a cross (how appropriate for a Christmas cookie!) with the tines of a fork. (Hint: don't lift up the fork but slide it out backward to keep the marks nice and crisp.) Bake for 12-13 minutes. Yields 4 dozen 2-inch cookies.

Peppermint Chiffon Pie

For years now, I have collected vintage cookbooks from tearooms of yesteryear, many of which are no longer in existence. This is a recipe I found in the 1964 *Woman's Exchange Cookbook, Volume 1*, published by the Woman's Exchange in Memphis, Tennessee, which was still operating at the time of this book's publication.

1/2 cup crushed peppermint candy (about 25 round peppermint candies, plus extra for garnish)
1/2 cup sugar, divided use
1 envelope gelatin (1/4-ounce size)
1-1/4 cups milk
3 pasteurized eggs*, yolks and whites divided
1/4 teaspoon salt
1 cup heavy whipping cream, whipped
1 premade graham cracker crust

In a small saucepan or double boiler, combine crushed candy, 1/4 cup of the sugar, gelatin, milk, lightly beaten egg yolks, and salt. Cook over low heat or in double boiler until gelatin dissolves and the peppermint candy has melted. Chill until partially set, about 1 hour. Beat egg whites until stiff peaks form, then gradually add remaining 1/4 cup of sugar. Fold into gelatin mixture, then fold in half of the whipped cream and pour into the graham cracker crust. Chill for several hours. Top pie with remaining whipped cream and crushed peppermints.

Pasteurized eggs only should be used in this recipe since they are only partially cooked.

Portuguese Honey Bread

On a visit to see family in Wisconsin a few years back, I went to a neighborhood garage sale down their street and came upon a copy of *Good Housekeeping's Family Christmas Book* for just 50 cents. Inside this magazine was a recipe for a gorgeous quick bread made in one of those old-fashioned copper-looking pans, this one featuring a rose design. I tracked down that exact pan on eBay and made this honey bread, which has a sophisticated spicy taste that pairs perfectly with a cup of tea.

The original recipe was designed to make three honey breads, but I reduced it to a single-sized recipe. And I was ridiculously happy when mine came out looking like the 1969 magazine photo!

3/4 cup butter or margarine, softened
1/2 cup molasses
1/4 cup honey
3/4 cup plus 2 tablespoons granulated sugar
2 tablespoons cold mashed potatoes
2 tablespoons cooking sherry
1/2 teaspoon ground cloves
1 teaspoon anise seed
1 tablespoon plus 1 teaspoon cinnamon
1/8 teaspoon black pepper
1/2 teaspoon baking soda
1/4 teaspoon baking powder
3-2/3 cups sifted all-purpose flour

This honey
bread has a
sophisticated
spicy taste that
pairs perfectly
with a cup of
tea.

Preheat oven
to 325 degrees. In large bowl of
an electric mixer, add butter, molasses, honey, and sugar and combine at medium speed
until fluffy. Add mashed potatoes, sherry, cloves, anise, cinnamon, pepper, baking soda,
and baking powder and beat till combined well.

Using low speed of mixer, add half of the flour. Mixture will be very thick, so add the
rest of the flour and mix well with a wooden spoon or a spatula just till combined.

Prepare 2-quart mold with cooking spray and add batter. Bake for 1-1/2 hours or until
a cake tester inserted in the center comes out clean. Bread should be coming away from
the sides of the mold.

Leave bread in mold and cool on wire rack for 10 minutes. Remove from mold and
serve warm, or let bread cool completely, wrap it tightly in foil, and let it "season" for several days at room temperature before giving as a gift. Yields 1 bread.

The easiest old recipes are often some of the best-tasting ones.

Potato Candy

I often wonder who was first to discover things. For instance, who was the first woman (for surely it was a woman) who thought, "You know, I believe I'll take these leftover mashed potatoes and turn them into candy!"

As a little girl, I first had potato candy when one of my aunts made it. That Christmas, she announced that she'd made a new treat out of mashed potatoes, and I remember all of us looking at her like she'd lost her mind. Then we ate some of it and became believers.

I'm reminded once again that the easiest old recipes are often some of the best-tasting ones. If someone in your family, especially the younger generation, has yet to experience potato candy, you know what you need to do.

1 small Russet potato, cooked and mashed
6 cups confectioners' sugar, plus more for dusting
1/4 cup creamy peanut butter

Place 1/2 cup of the mashed potatoes in bowl of electric mixer. Add confectioners' sugar 1 to 2 cups at a time, mixing well after each addition. Once all the sugar is incorporated, the mixture will be very stiff, with the texture of thick cookie dough.

Using sheets of wax paper lightly dusted with more confectioners' sugar, divide mixture in half. Loosely flatten into a rectangle, then use a rolling pin to press the mixture into a 1/4-inch-thick rectangle. I like to do the rolling between two sheets of wax paper to keep the mixture from sticking to my rolling pin, then I peel off the top layer to reveal a perfectly smooth dough. Using a knife, spread

a light, sheer layer of peanut butter onto mixture, spreading just to within a half inch of the edge. Starting at the longest side, roll the piece into a log shape. Once it is rolled up, secure the log tightly in the wax paper (as if it's one giant piece of candy), twist the ends of the paper to hold the log in place, and refrigerate until firm. Repeat with remaining half of mixture. Yields 3-4 dozen pieces of potato candy, depending on the size of your logs and slices. I tried them both large and small, and I liked the slices best when they were about 1-1/2 inches wide and 1/3 inch thick.

Tip: Make sure logs are good and cold before slicing, and slice the pieces with a sharp knife. Applying too much pressure on the log will result in misshapen, squishy-looking globs of candy that will still taste delicious, but if you're going for pretty—and aren't we all?—be sure to slice with a light hand.

Cards and Coasters and Doilies—Oh my!

O ne of the most fun and inexpensive Christmas collectibles to look for is a Christmas card or postcard. You can collect them by color (all red or pink or blue), by theme (the Holy Family, churches, reindeer, Santa), or by simply whatever catches your fancy.

What caught my fancy last year was a beautiful old Hallmark card I found at the Carriage House, my friend Nancy's charming antiques shop. I'd found some vintage Christmas cookie cutters and, to my delight, some beautiful rhinestone-embellished ladies' gloves. I definitely needed the gloves since I happen to write cozy mysteries about a character who loves vintage jewelry, particularly pieces featuring rhinestones. But before I could check out with my trea-

sures, I found a little basket containing old cards for just a dollar each. One, an old Hallmark card, depicted a pretty white Bible and bright-red poinsettias among some pine branches. I love that image so much. The Bible points me to the reason we celebrate Christmas, and poinsettias are so exotic and elegant.

Pieces of paper like that vintage card seem to

hold up quite well through the years, and they don't take up a lot of room. That's an important consideration now that I'm getting older and realize my heirs probably aren't going to be as thrilled with all this old junk as I am.

Along with Christmas cards, paper goods for the kitchen are other fun paper pieces to collect. On eBay once, I came across a stash of English paper napkins, coasters, and doilies. Some of the coasters were lightly padded and scalloped, a level of detail I certainly don't see in the throwaway paper goods of today.

Even greeting cards were prized at one time, as I sometimes run across old "vases" made of vintage greeting cards that have been crocheted together.

Antique malls occasionally have packages of old paper goods for the kitchen, and my favorite ones

Vintage cards seem to hold up quite well through the years.

Sincere greetings and every good
wish for a Merry Christmas
and a Happy New Year

Mary Lynyak

Elizabeth Zabrinskie
35 Spring St
Passaic, N.J.

are the waxed paper baking cups from England. I like mine so much, I refuse to use them for baking, but I don't mind using them for display and then rinsing them out afterward. (In this book, they're used to display the Mexican Spiced Nuts.)

Such items can be found at all the usual suspects—antique malls, thrift stores, eBay, Etsy—and if you're lucky, you might just inherit a few from a friend or family member.

Pumpkin Pie

One of my favorite "Christmas" songs is composer Leroy Anderson's 1948 "Sleigh Ride," which is said to have been penned as a wintertime tune, not a Christmas one. I was always intrigued by that line about the birthday party at the home of Farmer Gray, where they're passing around the coffee and the pumpkin pie. Can we assume that Farmer Gray had a good pumpkin harvest that year?

As velvety smooth as Johnny Mathis's voice

When I was growing up, pumpkin pie was something you ate at Thanksgiving, if at all, since we were dedicated pecan pie fans in my family. As an adult, however, I discovered that lots of folks consider pumpkin pie an appropriate Christmas food, and I happen to like pumpkin pie, too, so there you go.

One Saturday last year, I was at a thrift store in Rome (Georgia, not Italy) when I came across a 99-cent treasure that had long been on my wish list: the 1954 *Good and Easy Cook Book* from Betty Crocker. As I perused it, I was happy to find what must be one of the world's easiest pumpkin pie recipes. Not surprisingly, I had to update the can sizes a bit. And when it said *pastry for 9" one-crust pie*, I was pleased to note that while it pointed me to another page in the cookbook with a pie crust recipe, it did not technically say that I *had* to make the crust myself. I don't like to make pie crusts, and the Pet-Ritz people are our friends for a reason. Pre-made to the rescue!

This recipe gives a pie filling that's as velvety smooth as Johnny Mathis's voice when he's singing "Sleigh Ride."

1 (15-ounce) can pumpkin (I used Libby's)
1 (14-ounce) can sweetened condensed milk
1 large egg
1/2 teaspoon salt
1/2 teaspoon cinnamon
1/4 teaspoon nutmeg
1/4 teaspoon ginger
1 cup hot water
One unbaked 9-inch pie crust (deep-dish size)

Preheat oven to 375 degrees. Add pumpkin, sweetened condensed milk, egg, salt, spices, and water in bowl of electric mixer and combine well. Pour mixture into pie shell and cook for 50-55 minutes, just until a knife inserted along the edge of the filling comes out clean. When cool, garnish with whipped cream. ("If desired," said the Betty Crocker people. But who doesn't desire whipped cream?)

spritz Cookies

I usually start baking cookies by mid-November, preparing a different batch or two each weekend until Christmas. When Christmas week arrives, I have a nice variety of cookies to share and enjoy.

One year, I received a cookie press as a gift, and it was so quick and easy to use. I mixed up a simple dough for classic spritz cookies, and soon I was squirting perfectly shaped bits of dough onto my cookie sheets. According to whatscookingamerica.net, "The name comes from the German word *spritzen*, meaning 'to squirt,' because the soft dough is squirted or pushed through a cookie press to make fancy designs."

Old aluminum cookie presses from the early thirties sometimes show up in antique malls, and while I wouldn't mind having one of those purely for nostalgia, I love my modern cookie press with its easy-to-use trigger and clear barrel, which lets me know when I need to refill the cookie press with more dough. I pity the poor spritzers of yesteryear who were about to pull the trigger on a perfect cookie only to realize they were out of dough since they couldn't see through their nice aluminum gadget. A new cookie press is quite affordable and can be used for many years—and not just at Christmas.

While you can make chocolate-flavored spritz cookies, savory spritz cookies, and other variations, I prefer a classic butter recipe, perhaps embellished with sparkly sugar crystals in red or green. My favorite discs to use in the cookie press are in the shapes of flowers and Christmas trees, and these cookies turn out great no matter which shape you fancy.

1-1/2 cups butter
1 cup granulated sugar
1 egg
2 tablespoons milk
1 teaspoon vanilla extract
1/2 teaspoon almond extract
3-1/2 cups all-purpose flour
1 teaspoon baking powder

Preheat oven to 375 degrees. Cream butter and sugar, then add egg, milk, and extracts. Beat well. Combine the flour and baking powder, then add them to the creamed mixture and blend until a smooth dough forms. Do not chill. Place the dough in a cookie press and spritz dough onto greased cookie sheets. Bake cookies for 10-12 minutes or until lightly browned at the edges. Remove from cookie sheets and cool on wire rack. Yields 7-8 dozen cookies.

Stained Glass Cookies

Stained glass. What does that term mean to you? I see two things. First, I picture some of the beautiful stained glass artistry from the wonderful old homes where I live in Newnan, Georgia, known as the City of Homes. And second, I picture the stained glass in churches in both my hometown and around the world.

When my husband and I went to Normandy a few years ago, we stopped by the chapel of the church at Sainte-Mère-Église. The town was featured in the movie *The Longest Day*, and an iconic scene shows a paratrooper getting hung up at the pinnacle of the church tower. Inside the actual church, there is an amazing stained glass window depicting the soldier (in real life, he was American John Steele).

The stained glass I like best, though, is the stained glass at my church. On Christmas Eve, the soft colors cast a warm glow over the congregation as we gather to celebrate the arrival of the Christ Child.

So I'm grateful for stained glass, and I'm also grateful for Stained Glass Cookies, which I gather are much easier to make than the windows. For these cookies, I base my recipe on one from the excellent book *Cookie Craft* by Valerie Peterson and Janice Fryer. It's a book all about decorating those fancy royal icing cookies, which I've enjoyed making a time or two, and this recipe is now my go-to when I need a fool-proof sugar cookie for making something especially pretty. Stained Glass Cookies, though, are mostly about the technique and the candy, although I can tell you that these are as tasty as they are pretty, with the thin candy interior providing a satisfying crunch. Eat them reverently.

3 cups all-purpose flour
1/2 teaspoon salt
2 sticks of butter
1 cup sugar
1 large egg
2 teaspoons vanilla
1 (6.25-ounce) bag Life Savers candies (48 pieces)

Combine flour and salt in a bowl and set aside. Cream butter and sugar until fluffy, then add egg and vanilla and blend well. Slowly add flour and combine. Scoop dough onto a floured surface and divide into two portions. Flatten into discs between two pieces of wax paper, then chill the discs in the refrigerator for 30 minutes. Preheat oven to 350 degrees. Prepare cookie sheets with aluminum foil or parchment paper that is lightly sprayed with cooking spray.

Use a large* star-shaped cookie cutter to cut out dough. Then, use a smaller star-shaped cookie cutter to cut out a small star in the interior of this cookie. (Save this small scrap of dough so it can be rolled out again.) Carefully lift star outline to the prepared cookie sheet. Place one of the candies inside the star shape and adjust points of the star as needed. Space cookies two inches apart on cookie sheet and bake for 12-14 minutes or until tips of cookies are just starting to brown. Yields 4 dozen 3-1/2-inch cookies.

My large cookie cutter was 3-1/2 inches wide, and the smaller one was 1-3/4 inches wide.

Finding "New" Vintage Christmas Decor

SANTA MUGS
CHRISTMAS PARTY FAVOR
SWEETS. NUTS. CIGARETTES.
USE AS A TREE ORNAMENT
MADE IN JAPAN
TX-2114

I'd been prowling eBay for a while when I first came across the initials NOS. I wondered what a NOS was, and I soon learned that the initials stood for New Old Stock. These are items that are actually vintage but that were never sold at retail.

Similarly, MIP stands for Mint In Package, and if you find a vintage item that's MIP, you've really outdone yourself. That MIP designation would be important to, for instance, a collector who wants the box that originally came with that Madame Alexander doll they're buying. So some vintage items may be described as New Old Stock or Mint In Package or both.

But here's the thing about NOSes and MIPs: they can be HTF—Hard To Find.

Or not. I was browsing a local antiques shop one day when I came across an unopened package of miniature Santa mugs. The tiny Japanese mugs were similar to others I own, but the packaging itself intrigued me. The mugs were described as "Santa Mugs Christmas Party Favor—Sweets, Nuts, Cigarettes, Use as a Tree Ornament." Cigarettes? After all, nothing says Merry Christmas like "Light up, boys and girls!" It's a message you're not

going to see in this day and age, but in the fifties
and sixties, no one would have batted an eye at that.

Vintage boxes and packaging are fun to find, particularly because the graphics and prices give a snapshot of the day in which
they first appeared. I've even found old rolls of Scotch gift tape in
their original containers.

Old Christmas packaging can be as charming as the object
itself. One thrift store turned up a MIP 130-foot roll of Christmas

ribbon from Woolworth for just eighty-nine cents, only slightly more than the original price stamped on the package. It's one of my thriftiest Christmas finds, and I love that it's an everyday item that was preserved in its original condition.

Earlier this year, a run through the local Goodwill turned up three MIP sets of Christmas coasters, just fifty-nine cents each, and what charmed me most was their green price stickers from Walmart. The store hasn't used price stickers in years, and I believe the last time I saw the green ones was the late eighties or early nineties.

One of my favorite MIP items is a tiny card of jingling bells, acquired from a lovely Etsy seller whose shop is called A New Hampshire Attic. The delightful seller, Sara, even corresponded with me, emailing some images of vintage family recipes and sharing a cookbook that she knew I'd like.

If you're a fan of vintage Christmas items, too, it can be incredibly fun to come across "new" vintage items, just as long as you're not terribly IAH—In A Hurry—to find them.

One of my favorite MIP items is a tiny card of jingling bells.

Christmas Bells
3 TO CARD

CAN BE USED IN MANY DIFFERENT WAYS TO DECORATE CHRISTMAS PACKAGES, TREES, WREATHS, Etc.

MADE IN U.S.A.

© C. B. N. CO.
A CRITERION PRODUCT   BROOKLYN, N. Y.

Vanilla Cup Cakes

Over the years, I have saved a lot of the vintage images that I have found online, and one of them was a cute flyer advertising Betty Brite Bake Cups. The cups apparently came with recipes back in the day, and just as "cookie" was once spelled "cooky," the word "cupcakes" was once spelled "cup cakes."

When asked to make what I now call cupcakes, I tend to use a favorite chocolate cupcake recipe, but a few times in recent years, I wanted vanilla cupcakes and wasn't satisfied with the recipe I used. Then I found this one. I liked Betty Brite's recipe so much, this is now my go-to vanilla cupcake recipe.

Really, though, this was just an excuse to show off my VINTAGE CUPCAKE PICKS! (Sorry. I didn't mean to yell.) But aren't they charming? I found these at a local antique mall while enjoying a shopping day with my high school girlfriends Monicha and Patty. I like to think they brought me shopping luck.

2 cups all-purpose flour
1 cup sugar
1/4 teaspoon salt
3 teaspoons baking powder
1/4 cup shortening, melted
1 cup milk
1 egg, well beaten
1 teaspoon vanilla

Preheat oven to 375 degrees. Sift dry ingredients together. In separate bowl, combine melted shortening, milk, egg, and vanilla. Combine the two mixtures and blend. Use an ice cream scoop to fill baking cups about half full. Bake for 20 minutes. Yields 20 cupcakes.

Frost as desired with your favorite frosting recipe. (I like a simple buttercream frosting consisting of 1 cup softened butter, 4-1/2 cups confectioners' sugar, 1 teaspoon vanilla, and 4-5 tablespoons of milk.)

Need a go-to vanilla cupcake recipe?

In recent years, charming new products from Cavallini and Company (this page) and Martha Stewart (opposite) have featured vintage Christmas designs.

Vintage Christmas Reproductions

While I would always prefer a truly vintage Christmas item, I'm not above buying something new if it has The Look. And a few things I've come across look so convincingly vintage that I'm saving the packaging so my heirs (who, let's face it, won't care) won't confuse them with something new.

Cavallini and Company has been on my radar for years because of their lovely stationery that I've seen in bookstores and online. In 2018, they came out with a line of tea towels that could easily be mistaken for old ones. I got the one titled Christmas Noel, and I absolutely love it. It has Santas and pinecones and a wreath and a sled, and everything about it says Merry Christmas!

A similar design is featured on a line of dessert plates and mugs that Martha Stewart came out with in 2013. The pattern is called Vintage Holiday, and only the thickness of the ceramic and the glossiness of the plates reveal that these

aren't old pieces.

Do you like that whimsical collage-style pattern too? Then be on the lookout for vintage Christmas wrapping paper, which I usually come across when I'm not even looking for it. For the past several years, I've wrapped gifts with the Sleigh Hill Trading Company wrapping papers I found at T. J. Maxx. The vintage-look graphics are spot-on and just the thing I want to look at under my tree during the month of December. I also like to buy those large ninety-nine-cent "shopping" bags and use them as gift bags. Occasionally, I find them with pretty Christmas graphics and stock up.

Vintage-looking new decor also shows up at the major craft store chains, which in my neck of the woods include Hobby Lobby, Michaels, and Joann. In the past few years, I've found a cute plaque featuring Santa mugs and even some pink and turquoise reindeer figurines, which were welcome discoveries since the original reindeer are getting harder and harder to find. Some of these stores also have reproductions of those old-fashioned ceramic Christmas trees. I was lucky enough to find two small vintage ones for a dollar each at a thrift store last year, but I wouldn't have hesitated to buy a new one that looked vintage.

And while you're at the craft store, look for fabrics and scrapbooking papers with vintage Christmas designs. I've found adorable papers from Daisy D's and Carta Bella, and lots of fabric designers seem to have hopped on the vintage Christmas train.

Using vintage reproductions is a fun way to blend old and new vintage items, and I expect that even more stores will offer this decor in the years ahead.

Wonderland Sugar Cookies

I t's hard not to let the kid in you come out when it's time to make sugar cookies. I like to pull out a bunch of cookie cutters and different colors of sprinkles. I'm not big on changing the old recipes with a lot of froufrou, but as I've studied vintage magazine ads featuring Christmas cookies, I've learned that iced and sprinkled cookies are quite authentic, so if you're going to go a little overboard with the embellishments, this is the place to do it.

This recipe comes from a delightful 1952 booklet in my collection, *Aunt Jenny's Old-Fashioned Christmas Cookies and Other All-Time Favorites*.

1 cup shortening
2/3 cup sugar
1-1/4 teaspoons salt
2 teaspoons vanilla (or other flavored extracts)
2 unbeaten eggs
2-1/2 cups sifted all-purpose flour

Preheat oven to 375 degrees. Combine shortening, sugar, salt, vanilla, and eggs. Add the flour and mix well. Using a floured surface, roll out the dough to 1/8- or 1/4-inch thickness. Cut out various shapes with cookie cutters, place one inch apart on greased cookie sheets, and bake for 8-10 minutes. Ice and embellish cookies with sprinkles as desired. Yields about 4 dozen cookies.

Icing: For each color of icing, combine 1 cup of confectioners' sugar with 1-2 tablespoons of milk and tint with food coloring as desired.

Resources

SOME FAVORITE ANTIQUE STORES

Carriage House Country Antiques and Gifts, Senoia, GA; Habitat for Humanity ReStore, Newnan, GA; The Good Junk Co., Senoia, GA; Rockin' B Antiques, Newnan, GA; Treasures Lost & Found, Newnan, GA; Recycling the Past, Newnan, GA; ReThread Thrift Store, Carrollton, GA; Blake House Thrift Store, Carrollton, GA; Feathers and Twigs, Carrollton, GA; Apple Barrel Antiques, Bremen, GA; Kelly & Company Antiques, Fayetteville, GA: Ben's Antiques & Market, Douglasville, GA; Big Shanty Antiques, Marietta, GA; Park West Vintage, Marietta, GA; Cobb Antique Mall, Marietta, GA; and every Salvation Army and Goodwill store in existence.

ONLINE SELLERS

• Every junker knows to check sites like eBay, Etsy, Ruby Lane, and Goodwill.com, and I want to give a special thanks to Sara Tatham of ANewHampshireAttic on Etsy for her kindness and inspiration.
• Victorian Trading Co. (victoriantradingco.com) offers lovely reproductions of vintage Christmas wares and cards.
• Bethanylowe.com is a purveyor with beautiful vintage-looking Christmas wares inspired by the past.

BLOGS & WEBSITES

• On my tea blog, Teawithfriends.blogspot.com, I occasionally feature some of my vintage Christmas finds throughout the year.
• Relevanttealeaf.blogspot.com is the tea blog where my dear friend Phyllis Barkey in Michigan has, over Christmases past, shared hundreds of photos of clever tablescape ideas for Christmas teas and luncheons. (When you have a few hours to spare, visit her blog and type "Christmas tea" in the search box.)
• JenniferHayslip.com is the online home of a fellow Georgian I've never met, but I follow her blog and Instagram feed to see her charming pastel and Shabby Chic decor, including vintage Christmas decor.

• Facebook has quite a few vintage-loving groups I enjoy following, including one titled simply Vintage Christmas; Amy Barickman's Vintage Made Modern; and Retro Christmas Card Company, a source for delightfully retro Christmas cards and images.
• You can shop there only in your imagination now, but Wishbookweb.com is a site where you'll feel like a kid again as you peruse those fabulous Sears Christmas catalogs (as well as those of a few other retail giants) from your childhood. Great fun!

CRAFT SUPPLIES

• Fat Quarter Shop, Missouri Star Quilt Company, eQuilter.com, Hawthorne Supply Co., and Spoonflower.com are a few of the online fabric companies where I've found vintage Christmas designs.
• Are you a fellow paper crafter? I've found vintage Christmas prints on papers from Daisy D's, Carta Bella, and Tim Holtz. Search your favorite vendor for "vintage Christmas" and see what turns up.

MAGAZINES

• If I could keep only one Christmas magazine, it would be the Winter 2016 issue of *Flea Market Décor*, which is jam-packed with photos and ideas. Also a must-read: *Vintage Holiday* magazine issues from 2013-2018.

BOOKS

• *Christmas Vintage Holiday Graphics* by Jim Heimann (2005)
• *Holidays on Display* by William L. Bird, Jr. (2007)
• *Kitschmasland! Christmas Décor from the 1950s to the 1970s* by Travis Smith (2005)
• *The Complete Book of Retro Crafts* by Suzie Millions (2008)
• *Under the Tree: The Toys and Treats that Made Christmas Special*, 1930-1970 by Susan Waggoner (2007)
• *The Vintage Table* by Jacqueline deMontravel (2009)

Enjoyed this book? Please check out our other books!

Books by Angela McRae:

Dainty Dining   *A Year of Teatime Tales*   *Emeralds and Envy*

Books by Amelia Cronic and Deberah Williams:

*Gluten-free with
No Apologies*

*No Apologies Gluten-Free
Tailgates, Potlucks, Picnics & More*

CPSIA information can be obtained
at www.ICGtesting.com
Printed in the USA
BVHW061949021220
594501BV00002B/14

9 781087 923871